Your Medicare Benefits

This is the official government booklet with important information about the following:

★ The services and supplies Original Medicare covers

★ How much you pay

★ Where to get more information

ABOUT THIS BOOK

This booklet explains which health care services and supplies Medicare covers and how to get those benefits through Original Medicare Part A (Hospital Insurance) and Part B (Medical Insurance). It includes the rules for what specific benefits you can get and when. It also explains how much Medicare pays for each service and how much you pay. Finally, it gives you information on how to get help with any questions you may have.

If you have a question about an item or service that isn't listed in this booklet, visit www.medicare.gov and select, "Find Out What Medicare Covers." You can also call 1-800-MEDICARE (1-800-633-4227). TTY users should call 1-877-486-2048.

There are other Medicare publications available with more detailed information on many of the items and services mentioned in this booklet. For a list of specific publications, see page 44–46.

"Your Medicare Benefits" isn't a legal document. The official Medicare Program legal guidance is contained in the relevant laws, regulations, and rulings.

Table of Contents

Note: The information in this booklet was correct when it was printed. Changes may occur. To find out if the information has been updated, call 1-800-MEDICARE (1-800-633-4227). TTY users should call 1-877-486-2048.

List of Topics

Blue words in the text are defined on pages 49–51.

2

List of Topics

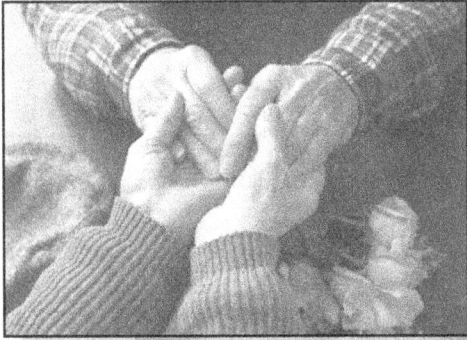

List of What Original Medicare Covers

The information starting on the next page explains the following:

- Services and supplies covered by Original Medicare
- Conditions and limits for coverage
- How much you pay

As you read this booklet, keep these two points in mind:

1. Unless otherwise noted, in 2010, you pay an annual $155 deductible for Part B-covered services and supplies before Medicare begins to pay its share, depending on the service or supply.

2. Actual amounts you pay may be higher if doctors, other health care providers, or suppliers don't accept assignment, depending on the service or supply.

The information about services and supplies listed in these charts applies to all people with Original Medicare. If you're enrolled in a Medicare Advantage Plan (like an HMO or PPO) or other Medicare health plan, you have the same basic benefits, but the rules vary by plan. Some services and supplies may not be listed because the coverage depends on where you live. To find out more, visit www.medicare.gov, or call 1-800-MEDICARE (1-800-633-4227). TTY users should call 1-877-486-2048.

Preventive Services

There is a picture of an apple next to each preventive service that Medicare covers. These services can keep you from getting certain illnesses, or can find health problems early, when treatment works best. Talk with your doctor about which preventive services Medicare will cover for you.

Abdominal Aortic Aneurysm Screening

Medicare Part B covers a one-time screening ultrasound for people at risk. You're considered at risk if you have a family history of abdominal aortic aneurysms, or you're a man age 65 to 75 and have smoked at least 100 cigarettes in your lifetime. Medicare only covers this screening if you get a referral for it as a result of your "Welcome to Medicare" physical exam.

In 2010, YOU pay 20% of the Medicare-approved amount for the doctor's services. In a hospital outpatient setting, you pay a copayment. The Part B deductible doesn't apply.

Acupuncture

Medicare doesn't cover acupuncture.

Ambulance Services

Medicare Part B covers emergency ground ambulance transportation when you need to be transported to a hospital or skilled nursing facility for medically-necessary services, and transportation in any other vehicle could endanger your health.

Medicare will pay for emergency ambulance transportation in an airplane or helicopter to a hospital if you require immediate and rapid ambulance transportation that ground transportation can't provide. Medicare will only cover ambulance services (ground or air) to the nearest appropriate medical facility that's able to give you the care you need.

In some cases, Medicare may pay for limited non-emergency ambulance transportation if you have orders from your doctor saying that ambulance transportation is necessary because of your medical condition.

In 2010, YOU pay 20% of the Medicare-approved amount. All ambulance suppliers must accept assignment.

Ambulatory Surgical Centers

Blue words in the text are defined on pages 49–51.

Medicare Part B covers approved surgical procedures provided in an ambulatory surgical center.

In 2010, YOU pay 20% of the Medicare-approved amount (except for screening flexible sigmoidoscopies and screening colonoscopies, for which you pay 25%). You pay all facility charges for procedures Medicare doesn't allow in ambulatory surgical centers.

6

Section 1: List of What Original Medicare Covers

Anesthesia

Medicare Part A covers anesthesia services provided by a hospital for an inpatient. Medicare Part B covers anesthesia services provided by a hospital for an outpatient or by a freestanding ambulatory surgical center for a patient.

> **In 2010, YOU pay** 20% of the Medicare-approved amount for the anesthesia services provided by a doctor or certified registered nurse anesthetist. The anesthesia service must be associated with the underlying medical or surgical service.

Artificial Limbs and Eyes

Medicare Part B covers artificial limbs and eyes when ordered by a doctor.

> **In 2010, YOU pay** 20% of the Medicare-approved amount.

Blood

B

Medicare Part A covers blood you get as an inpatient. Medicare Part B covers blood you get as a hospital outpatient.

> **In 2010, YOU pay** either the provider costs for the first 3 units of blood you get in a calendar year, or you must have the blood replaced (donated by you or someone else) if the provider has to buy blood for you. In most cases, the provider doesn't have to pay the blood bank for the blood, and you won't have to pay for it or replace it.

Blood Processing and Handling

Hospitals generally charge for blood processing and handling, whether the blood is donated or purchased. Medicare Part A covers this service for an inpatient. Medicare Part B covers this service for an outpatient.

> **In 2010, YOU pay** a copayment for blood processing and handling services for every unit of blood you get as a hospital outpatient.

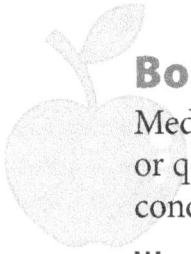

Bone Mass Measurement (Bone Density)

Medicare Part B covers bone mass measurements ordered by a doctor or qualified practitioner if you meet one or more of the following conditions:

Women

You're at clinical risk for osteoporosis, based on your medical history and other findings

Men and Women

- Your X-rays show possible osteoporosis, osteopenia, or vertebrae fractures.
- You're on prednisone or steroid-type drugs or are planning to begin such treatment.
- You have been diagnosed with primary hyperparathyroidism.
- You're being monitored to see if your osteoporosis drug therapy is working.

The test is covered once every 24 months for qualified individuals and more often if medically necessary.

In 2010, YOU pay 20% of the Medicare-approved amount. In a hospital outpatient setting, you pay a copayment.

Braces (arm, leg, back, and neck)

Medicare Part B covers arm, leg, back, and neck braces.

In 2010, YOU pay 20% of the Medicare-approved amount.

Breast Prostheses

Medicare Part B covers external breast prostheses (including a post-surgical bra) after a mastectomy. Medicare Part A or Part B covers surgically implanted breast prostheses depending on whether the surgery takes place in an inpatient or outpatient setting.

In 2010, YOU pay 20% of the Medicare-approved amount for the doctor's services and the external breast prostheses. For surgeries to implant breast prostheses in a hospital inpatient setting covered under Part A, see Hospital Care (Inpatient) on page 23. For surgeries to implant breast prostheses in a hospital outpatient setting covered under Part B, see Outpatient Hospital Services on page 28.

Canes/Crutches

C

Medicare Part B covers canes and crutches. Medicare doesn't cover white canes for the blind. For more information, see Durable Medical Equipment on pages 17–18.

In 2010, YOU pay 20% of the Medicare-approved amount.

Cardiac Rehabilitation Program

Medicare Part B covers comprehensive programs that include exercise, education, and counseling for patients whose doctor referred them and who had any of the following:

- A heart attack in the last 12 months
- Coronary bypass surgery
- Current stable angina pectoris (chest pain)
- Heart valve repair/replacement
- Angioplasty (a medical procedure used to open a blocked artery) or coronary stenting (device used to keep an artery open)
- A heart or heart-lung transplant

Medicare Part B also covers intensive cardiac rehabilitation (ICR) programs that, like cardiac rehabilitation (CR) programs, include exercise, education, and counseling for patients whose doctor referred them and who had any of the conditions listed above. ICR programs are typically more rigorous or more intense than CR programs.

These programs may be provided in a hospital outpatient setting or in doctor-directed clinics.

> Blue words in the text are defined on pages 49–51.

In 2010, YOU pay 20% of the Medicare-approved amount for the doctor's services. In a hospital outpatient setting, you pay a copayment.

Cardiovascular Disease Screenings

Medicare Part B covers screening tests for cholesterol, lipid, and triglyceride levels every 5 years to help you prevent a heart attack or stroke.

In 2010, YOU pay $0 for this test.

Chemotherapy

Medicare Part A covers chemotherapy for cancer patients who are hospital inpatients. Medicare Part B covers chemotherapy for hospital outpatients or patients in a doctor's office or freestanding clinic.

In 2010, YOU pay a copayment for chemotherapy covered under Part B in a hospital outpatient setting. For chemotherapy given in a doctor's office or freestanding clinic, you pay 20% of the Medicare-approved amount. For chemotherapy in the hospital inpatient setting covered under Part A, see Hospital Care (Inpatient) on page 23.

Chiropractic Services

Medicare Part B covers manipulation of the spine if medically necessary to correct a subluxation (when one or more of the bones of your spine move out of position) when provided by a chiropractor or other qualified provider.

In 2010, YOU pay 20% of the Medicare-approved amount. You pay all costs for any services or tests ordered by a chiropractor.

Clinical Research Studies

Clinical research studies test different types of medical care, like how well a cancer drug works. These studies help doctors and researchers see if new care works and if it's safe. Medicare Part A and/or Part B covers some costs, like doctor visits and tests, in a qualifying clinical research study.

In 2010, YOU pay the part of the payment that you would normally pay for covered services.

Colorectal Cancer Screening

Medicare Part B covers several colorectal cancer screening tests to help find precancerous growths and help prevent or find cancer early. All people 50 and older with Medicare are covered. However, there's no minimum age for having a colonoscopy.

Barium Enema: When this test is used instead of a flexible sigmoidoscopy or colonoscopy, Medicare covers the test once every 48 months for people age 50 or over and once every 24 months for people at high risk for colorectal cancer.

In 2010, YOU pay 20% of the Medicare-approved amount for the doctor's services. In a hospital outpatient setting, you pay a copayment. The Part B deductible doesn't apply.

Blue words in the text are defined on pages 49–51.

Colorectal Cancer Screening (continued)

Colonoscopy: Medicare covers this test once every 24 months if you're at high risk for colorectal cancer. If you aren't at high risk for colorectal cancer, Medicare covers the test once every 120 months or 48 months after a screening flexible sigmoidoscopy.

> **In 2010, YOU pay** 20% of the Medicare-approved amount for the doctor's services. In a hospital outpatient setting, you pay a copayment. The Part B deductible **doesn't** apply. However, if a screening test results in the biopsy or removal of a lesion or growth, the procedure is considered diagnostic, and the Part B deductible **does** apply.

Fecal Occult Blood Test: Medicare covers this lab test once every 12 months for people 50 or older.

> **In 2010, YOU pay** $0 for this test, but you generally have to pay 20% of the Medicare-approved amount for the doctor's visit. The Part B deductible doesn't apply

Flexible Sigmoidoscopy: Medicare covers this test once every 48 months for most people 50 or older. For those not at high risk, Medicare covers this test 120 months after a previous screening colonoscopy.

> **In 2010, YOU pay** 20% of the Medicare-approved amount for the doctor's services. In a hospital outpatient setting, you pay a copayment. The Part B deductible **doesn't** apply. However, if a screening test results in the biopsy or removal of a lesion or growth, the procedure is considered diagnostic, and the Part B deductible **does** apply.

Note: If you get a screening flexible sigmoidoscopy or screening colonoscopy in an outpatient hospital setting or an ambulatory surgical center, you pay 25% of the Medicare-approved amount.

Commode Chairs

Medicare Part B covers commode chairs that your doctor orders for use in your home if you're confined to your bedroom. For more information, see Durable Medical Equipment on pages 17–18.

> **In 2010, YOU pay** 20% of the Medicare-approved amount.

Cosmetic Surgery

Medicare generally doesn't cover cosmetic surgery unless it's needed because of accidental injury or to improve the function of a malformed body part. Medicare covers breast reconstruction if you had a mastectomy because of breast cancer.

Custodial Care (help with activities of daily living, like bathing, dressing, using the bathroom, and eating)

Medicare doesn't cover custodial care when it's the only kind of care you need. Care is considered custodial when it helps you with activities of daily living or personal needs and could be done safely and reasonably by people without professional skills or training.

Defibrillator (Implantable Automatic)

D

Medicare Part A or Part B covers defibrillators for certain people diagnosed with heart failure depending on whether the surgery takes place in a hospital inpatient or outpatient setting.

> **In 2010, YOU pay** 20% of the Medicare-approved amount for the doctor's services. You pay a copayment but no more than the Part A hospital stay deductible if you get the defibrillator as a hospital outpatient. For surgeries to implant defibrillators in the hospital inpatient setting covered under Part A, see Hospital Care (Inpatient) on page 23.

Dental Services

Medicare doesn't cover routine dental care or most dental procedures such as cleanings, fillings, tooth extractions, dentures, dental plates, or other dental devices. Medicare Part A will pay for certain dental services that you get when you're in a hospital. Medicare Part A can pay for hospital stays if you need to have emergency or complicated dental procedures, even when the dental care isn't covered.

Blue words in the text are defined on pages 49–51.

Section 1: List of What Original Medicare Covers

Diabetes Screenings

Medicare Part B covers tests to check for diabetes. These tests are available if you have any of the following risk factors: high blood pressure, dyslipidemia (history of abnormal cholesterol and triglyceride levels), obesity, or a history of high blood sugar. Medicare also covers these tests if two or more of the following apply to you:

- Age 65 or older
- Overweight
- Family history of diabetes (parents, brothers, sisters)
- A history of gestational diabetes (diabetes during pregnancy) or delivery of a baby weighing more than 9 pounds

Based on the results of these tests, you may be eligible for up to two diabetes screenings every year.

> **In 2010, YOU pay** $0 for this test, but you generally have to pay 20% of the Medicare-approved amount for the doctor's visit.

Diabetes Supplies and Services

Medicare Part B covers some diabetes supplies, including the following:

- Blood sugar (glucose) test strips
- Blood sugar monitor
- Lancet devices and lancets
- Glucose control solutions for checking test strip and monitor accuracy

There may be limits on how much or how often you get these supplies. For more information, see Durable Medical Equipment on page 17.

> **In 2010, YOU pay** 20% of the Medicare-approved amount.

Insulin: Medicare Part B doesn't cover insulin (unless used with an insulin pump), insulin pens, syringes, needles, alcohol swabs, or gauze. Insulin and certain medical supplies used to inject insulin, such as syringes, gauze, and alcohol swabs may be covered under Part D. If you use an external insulin pump, insulin and the pump may be covered as durable medical equipment. See Durable Medical Equipment (DME) on pages 17–18.

> **In 2010, YOU pay** 100% for insulin unless used with an insulin pump (then you pay 20% of the Medicare-approved amount) and 100% for syringes and needles, unless you have Part D.

Diabetes Supplies and Services (continued)

Therapeutic Shoes or Inserts: Medicare Part B covers therapeutic shoes or inserts for people with diabetes who have severe diabetic foot disease. The doctor who treats your diabetes must certify your need for therapeutic shoes or inserts. The shoes and inserts must be prescribed by a podiatrist or other qualified doctor and provided by a podiatrist, orthotist, prosthetist, or pedorthist. Medicare helps pay for one pair of therapeutic shoes and inserts per calendar year. Shoe modifications may be substituted for inserts. Medicare covers the fitting of the shoes or inserts for the shoes.

In 2010, YOU pay 20% of the Medicare-approved amount.

Medicare covers these diabetes services:

Diabetes Self-Management Training: Medicare Part B covers diabetes outpatient self-management training to teach you to manage your diabetes. It includes education about how you monitor your blood sugar, diet, exercise, and insulin. If you've been diagnosed with diabetes, Medicare may cover up to 10 hours of initial diabetes self-management training. You may also qualify for up to 2 hours of follow-up training each year if the following conditions are met:

- It's provided in a group of 2 to 20 people.*
- It lasts for at least 30 minutes.
- It takes place in a calendar year after the year you got your initial training.
- Your doctor or a qualified provider ordered it as part of your plan of care.

* Some exceptions apply if no group session is available or if your doctor or qualified provider says you have special needs that prevent you from participating in group training.

In 2010, YOU pay 20% of the Medicare-approved amount.

Yearly Eye Exam: Medicare Part B covers a yearly eye exam for diabetic retinopathy by an eye doctor who is legally allowed by the state to do the test.

In 2010, YOU pay 20% of the Medicare-approved amount for the doctor's services. In a hospital outpatient setting, you pay a copayment.

Blue words in the text are defined on pages 49–51.

Diabetes Supplies and Services (continued)

Foot Exam: Medicare Part B covers a foot exam every 6 months for people with diabetic peripheral neuropathy and loss of protective sensations, as long as you haven't seen a foot care professional for another reason between visits.

> **In 2010, YOU pay** 20% of the Medicare-approved amount for the doctor's services. In a hospital outpatient setting, you pay a copayment.

Glaucoma Tests: See page 20.

Medical Nutrition Therapy Services: See page 27.

Diagnostic Tests, X-rays, and Clinical Laboratory Services

Medicare Part B covers diagnostic tests like CT scans, MRIs, EKGs, and X-rays when your doctor or health care provider orders them as part of treating a medical problem. Medicare also covers clinical diagnostic laboratory services provided by certified laboratories enrolled in Medicare. Diagnostic tests and lab services are done to help your doctor diagnose or rule out a suspected illness or condition. Medicare doesn't cover most routine screening tests, like checking your hearing. Medicare covers some preventive tests and screenings to help prevent, find, or manage a medical problem. For more information, see Preventive Services on page 33.

> **In 2010, YOU pay** 20% of the Medicare-approved amount for covered diagnostic tests and X-rays done in a doctor's office or independent testing facility. You pay a copayment for diagnostic tests and X-rays in the hospital outpatient setting. You pay $0 for Medicare-covered lab services.

Section 1: List of What Original Medicare Covers

Dialysis (Kidney) Services and Supplies

Medicare covers some kidney dialysis services and supplies for people with End-Stage Renal Disease (ESRD).

Inpatient dialysis treatments: Medicare Part A covers dialysis if you're admitted to the hospital for special care. See Hospital Care (Inpatient) on page 23.

Outpatient maintenance dialysis treatments: Medicare Part B covers dialysis if you need regular treatments, and you get treatments in any Medicare-approved dialysis facility.

> **In 2010, YOU pay** 20% of the Medicare-approved amount.

Certain home dialysis support services: Medicare Part B covers visits by trained dialysis workers to check on your home dialysis, to help in dialysis emergencies when needed, and to check your dialysis equipment and hemodialysis water supply.

> **In 2010, YOU pay** 20% of the Medicare-approved amount. Only dialysis facilities can furnish home dialysis support services.

Certain drugs for home dialysis: Medicare Part B covers heparin, the antidote for heparin when medically necessary, and topical anesthetics.

> **In 2010, YOU pay** 20% of the Medicare-approved amount, if you deal with a supplier. If you deal with the dialysis facility, these drugs are included in the cost of dialysis.

Erythropoiesis–stimulating Agents: Medicare covers agents like Epogen®, Epoetin alfa, Aranesp®, or Darbepoetinalfa to treat anemia if you have End-Stage Renal Disease.

> **In 2010, YOU pay** 20% of the Medicare-approved amount.

Self-dialysis training: Medicare Part B covers training for you and the person helping you with your home dialysis treatments.

> **In 2010, YOU pay** 20% of the Medicare-approved amount.

Blue words in the text are defined on pages 49–51.

Home dialysis equipment and supplies: Medicare Part B covers equipment and supplies like alcohol, wipes, sterile drapes, rubber gloves, and scissors.

> **In 2010, YOU pay** 20% of the Medicare-approved amount. If you deal with a dialysis facility, the cost of home dialysis equipment and supplies is included in the cost of dialysis. If you deal with a medical supply company, it (not the dialysis facility) must accept assignment.

Section 1: List of What Original Medicare Covers

Doctor's Services

Medicare Part B covers medically-necessary services or covered preventive services you get from your doctor in his or her office, in a hospital, in a skilled nursing facility, in your home, or any other location.

Medicare doesn't cover routine physicals, except the one-time "Welcome to Medicare" physical exam. See page 29. Medicare covers some preventive tests and screenings. See Preventive Services on page 33.

In 2010, YOU pay 20% of the Medicare-approved amount.

Drugs

See Prescription Drugs (Outpatient) on pages 31–32.

Durable Medical Equipment (DME)

Medicare Part B covers Durable Medical Equipment (DME) that your doctor prescribes for use in your home. Only your doctor can prescribe medical equipment for you. Durable medical equipment meets the following criteria:

- Durable (long lasting)
- Used for a medical reason
- Not usually useful to someone who isn't sick or injured
- Used in your home

The DME that Medicare covers includes, but isn't limited to, the following:
- Air-fluidized beds
- Blood sugar monitors
- Canes (white canes for the blind aren't covered)
- Commode chairs
- Crutches
- Dialysis machines
- Home oxygen equipment and supplies
- Hospital beds
- Infusion pumps (and some medicines used in infusion pumps if considered reasonable and necessary)
- Nebulizers (and some medicines used in nebulizers if considered reasonable and necessary)
- Patient lifts (to lift patient from bed or wheelchair by hydraulic operation)
- Suction pumps
- Traction equipment
- Walkers
- Wheelchairs

Durable Medical Equipment (DME) (continued)

Make sure your doctor or supplier is enrolled in Medicare. Doctors and other suppliers have to meet strict standards to enroll and stay enrolled in Medicare.

If your doctor or supplier isn't enrolled, Medicare won't pay the claim submitted by your doctor or supplier, even if your supplier is a large chain or department store that sells more than just durable medical equipment.

> **In 2010, YOU pay** 20% of the Medicare-approved amount. Medicare pays for different kinds of DME in different ways; some equipment must be rented, other equipment may be purchased, and you may choose to rent or buy some equipment. If a DME supplier doesn't accept assignment, Medicare doesn't limit how much the supplier can charge you. You also may have to pay the entire bill (your share and Medicare's share) at the time you get the DME.

Note: Ask if the supplier is a participating supplier in the Medicare Program before you get durable medical equipment. If the supplier is a participating supplier, it **must** accept assignment. If the supplier is enrolled in Medicare but isn't "participating," it may choose not to accept assignment. To find suppliers who accept assignment, visit www.medicare.gov, and select, "Find Suppliers of Medical Equipment in Your Area." You can also call 1-800-MEDICARE (1-800-633-4227). TTY users should call 1-877-486-2048.

EKG Screening

Medicare Part B covers a one-time screening EKG if you get a referral for it as a result of your one-time "Welcome to Medicare" physical exam. See Physical Exams on page 29. An EKG is also covered as a diagnostic test. See page 15.

> **In 2010, YOU pay** 20% of the Medicare-approved amount.

Emergency Department Services

Medicare Part B covers emergency department services. Emergency services may be covered in foreign countries only in rare circumstances. For more information, see Travel on pages 40–41. A medical emergency is when you believe that you have an injury or illness that requires immediate medical attention to prevent a disability or death.

> **In 2010, YOU pay** a copayment for each emergency department visit unless you're admitted to the same hospital for the same condition within 3 days of your emergency department visit. When you go to an emergency department, you pay a copayment for each hospital service. You also pay 20% of the Medicare-approved amount for the doctor's services.

Blue words in the text are defined on pages 49–51.

Section 1: List of What Original Medicare Covers

Equipment

See Durable Medical Equipment on pages 17–18.

Eye Exams

Medicare doesn't cover routine eye exams (refractions) for eye glasses/contact lenses. Medicare covers some preventive and diagnostic eye exams:

- See yearly eye exams under Diabetes Supplies and Services on pages 13–15.
- See Glaucoma Tests on page 20.
- See Macular Degeneration on page 24.

Eyeglasses/Contact Lenses

Generally, Medicare doesn't cover eyeglasses or contact lenses. However, **following cataract surgery with an implanted intraocular lens**, Medicare Part B helps pay for corrective lenses (eyeglasses or contact lenses).

> **In 2010, YOU pay** 100%, in general. You pay 20% of the Medicare-approved amount for one pair of eyeglasses or contact lenses after each cataract surgery with an intraocular lens. You pay any additional cost for upgraded frames.

Eye Refractions

Medicare doesn't cover routine eye refractions for eye glasses/contacts. See Eye Exams.

Flu Shots

Medicare Part B normally covers one flu shot per flu season in the fall or winter.

> **In 2010, YOU pay** $0 for a flu shot if the doctor or supplier accepts assignment for administering the shot. If the doctor or supplier doesn't accept assignment, you pay 20% of the Medicare-approved amount.

Note: Medicare Part B also covers the administration of the 2009 H1N1 flu shot. You pay $0 if your doctor or other health care provider accepts assignment for administering the shot.

F

Foot Care

Medicare Part B covers the services of a podiatrist (foot doctor) for medically-necessary treatment of injuries or diseases of the foot (such as hammer toe, bunion deformities, and heel spurs), but it doesn't cover routine foot care. See Therapeutic Shoes and Foot Exam under Diabetes Supplies and Services on pages 13–15.

In 2010, YOU pay 100% for routine foot care, in most cases. You pay 20% of the Medicare-approved amount for medically-necessary treatment provided by a doctor. In a hospital outpatient setting, you pay a copayment for medically-necessary treatment.

G

Glaucoma Tests

Medicare Part B covers a glaucoma test once every 12 months for people at high risk for glaucoma. This includes people with diabetes, a family history of glaucoma, African Americans 50 and older, and Hispanic Americans 65 and older. The screening must be done or supervised by an eye doctor who is legally allowed to do this test in your state.

In 2010, YOU pay 20% of the Medicare-approved amount for the doctor's services. In a hospital outpatient setting, you pay a copayment.

H

Health Education/Wellness Programs

Medicare generally doesn't cover health education and wellness programs. However, Medicare does cover medical nutrition therapy for people with diabetes or kidney disease and diabetes education for people with diabetes (see page 27), counseling to stop smoking (see page 38), and a one-time "Welcome to Medicare" physical exam (see page 29).

Hearing and Balance Exams/Hearing Aids

In some cases, Medicare Part B covers diagnostic hearing and balance exams. Medicare doesn't cover routine hearing exams, hearing aids, or exams for fitting hearing aids.

In 2010, YOU pay 100% for routine exams and hearing aids. You pay 20% of the Medicare-approved amount for the doctor's services for covered exams. In a hospital outpatient setting, you pay a copayment.

Blue words in the text are defined on pages 49–51.

20

Hepatitis B Shots

Medicare Part B covers this shot for people at high or medium risk for Hepatitis B. Your risk for Hepatitis B increases if you have hemophilia, End-Stage Renal Disease (permanent kidney failure requiring dialysis or a kidney transplant), or a condition that lowers your resistance to infection. Other factors may also increase your risk for Hepatitis B. Check with your doctor to see if you're at high or medium risk for Hepatitis B.

In 2010, YOU pay 20% of the Medicare-approved amount for Hepatitis B shots given in a doctor's office. You pay a copayment for a Hepatitis B shot given in a hospital outpatient setting.

HIV Screening

Starting December 8, 2009, Medicare Part B covers HIV screening for people with Medicare who are pregnant and people at increased risk for the infection, including anyone who asks for the test. Medicare covers this test once every 12 months or up to three times during a pregnancy.

In 2010, YOU pay $0 for the test, but you generally pay 20% of the Medicare-approved amount for the doctor's visit.

Home Health Services

You can use your home health benefits under Medicare Part A and/or Part B if you meet all the following conditions:
- Your doctor decides you need medical care at home and makes a plan for it.
- You need at least one of the following, qualifying skilled services:
  - Intermittent skilled nursing care (other than just drawing blood)
  - Physical therapy
  - Speech-language pathology services
  - Continued occupational therapy
- The home health agency caring for you is Medicare-certified.
- You must be homebound, meaning that you're normally unable to leave home unassisted. When you do leave the home, it's a considerable and taxing effort. A person may leave home for medical treatment or short, infrequent absences for non-medical reasons, such as a trip to attend religious services. You can still get home health care if you attend adult day care.

Note: Home health services may also include part-time or intermittent home health aide services, medical social services, medical supplies, durable medical equipment (see pages 17–18), and an injectable osteoporosis drug.

In 2010, YOU pay $0 for all covered home health visits.

Home Health Services (continued)

Osteoporosis Drugs for Women: Medicare Part A and B help pay for an injectable drug for osteoporosis in women who are eligible for Medicare Part B, meet the criteria for Medicare home health services, and have a bone fracture that a doctor certifies was related to post-menopausal osteoporosis. You must also be certified by a doctor as unable to learn or unable to give yourself the drug by injection, and that family and/or caregivers are unable or unwilling to give the drug by injection. Medicare covers the visit by a home health nurse to give the drug.

> **In 2010, YOU pay** 20% of the Medicare-approved amount for the cost of the drug. You pay $0 for the home health nurse visit to give the drug.

Hospice Care

Medicare Part A covers hospice care if you meet all of the following conditions:

- You are eligible for Medicare Part A.
- Your doctor certifies that you're terminally ill and probably have less than 6 months to live.*
- You accept palliative care (for comfort) instead of care to cure your illness.
- You sign a statement choosing hospice care instead of routine Medicare-covered benefits for your terminal illness.

* In a Medicare-approved hospice, nurse practitioners aren't permitted to certify the patient's terminal diagnosis, but after a doctor certifies the diagnosis, the nurse practitioner can serve in place of an attending doctor.

You can continue to get hospice care as long as the hospice medical director or hospice doctor recertifies that you're terminally ill.

Inpatient Respite Care: Respite care is inpatient care given to a hospice patient so that the usual caregiver can rest. You can stay in a Medicare-approved facility, such as a hospice facility, hospital, or nursing home, up to 5 days each time you get respite care. Medicare will still pay for covered benefits for any health problems that aren't related to your terminal illness.

> **In 2010, YOU pay** $0 for hospice care. You may need to pay a copayment of up to $5 for outpatient prescription drugs for symptom control or pain relief. Medicare doesn't cover room and board when you get hospice care in your home or another facility where you live (like a nursing home).

Blue words in the text are defined on pages 49–51.

Hospice Care (continued)

In certain cases, if the hospice staff determines that you need inpatient care in a hospice facility or your caregiver needs a short period of respite, Medicare covers the costs for room and board. You pay 5% of the Medicare-approved amount for inpatient respite care.

Hospital Bed

See Durable Medical Equipment on pages 17–18.

Hospital Care (Inpatient)

For Outpatient Services, see page 28.

Medicare Part A covers inpatient hospital care when **all** of the following are true:

- A doctor says you need inpatient hospital care to treat your illness or injury.
- You need the kind of care that can be given only in a hospital.
- The hospital accepts Medicare.
- The Utilization Review Committee of the hospital approves your stay while you're in the hospital.

Medicare-covered hospital services include the following: a semiprivate room, meals, general nursing, and other hospital services and supplies. This includes care you get in critical access hospitals and inpatient mental health care. See pages 25–26. This doesn't include private-duty nursing, a television or a telephone in your room, and personal care items like razors or slipper socks. It also doesn't include a private room, unless medically necessary.

> **In 2010, YOU pay** for each benefit period:
>
> Days 1 - 60: $1,100 deductible
>
> Days 61 - 90: $275 coinsurance each day
>
> Days 91 - 150: $550 coinsurance each day
>
> Beyond 150 days: all costs
>
> You pay for private-duty nursing, a television, or a telephone in your room. You pay for a private room unless it's medically necessary. For more information about benefit periods and lifetime reserve days, see pages 49–50.

Kidney (Dialysis)

See Dialysis on page 16.

Kidney Disease Education

Starting January 1, 2010, Medicare covers Kidney Disease Education services if you have stage IV chronic kidney disease. Kidney Disease Education teaches you things you can do to take the best possible care of your kidneys and gives you information you need to make informed decisions about your care. Medicare covers up to six sessions of Kidney Disease Education services when given by a doctor, certain non-doctor providers, or a rural provider.

> **In 2010, YOU pay** 20% of the Medicare-approved amount per session if you get the service from a doctor or other health care provider.

Laboratory Services (Clinical)

Medicare Part B covers medically-necessary diagnostic lab services that are ordered by your treating doctor. Services include certain blood tests, urinalysis, some screening tests, and more. They must be provided by a laboratory that meets Medicare requirements. For more information, see Diagnostic Tests on page 15.

> **In 2010, YOU pay** $0 for Medicare-approved lab services.

Macular Degeneration

Medicare Part B covers certain diagnoses and treatment of diseases and conditions of the eye for some patients with age-related macular degeneration (AMD) like ocular photodynamic therapy with verteporfin (Visudyne®).

> **In 2010, YOU pay** 20% of the Medicare-approved amount for the doctor's services. In a hospital outpatient setting, you pay a copayment.

Blue words in the text are defined on pages 49-51.

Mammograms

Medicare Part B covers a screening mammogram once every 12 months (11 full months must have gone by from the last screening) for all women with Medicare who are 40 and older. You can also get one baseline mammogram between 35 and 39.

In 2010, YOU pay 20% of the Medicare-approved amount. The Part B deductible doesn't apply.

Medicare Part B covers diagnostic mammograms when medically necessary.

In 2010, YOU pay 20% of the Medicare-approved amount.

Medical Nutrition Therapy Services

See Nutrition Therapy Services (Medical) on page 27.

Mental Health Care

Medicare Part A and Part B cover mental health services in a variety of settings.

Inpatient Mental Health Care: Medicare Part A covers inpatient mental health care services. These services can be given in hospitals, including specialized psychiatric units, or specialized psychiatric hospitals. Medicare helps pay for inpatient mental health services in the same way that it pays for all other inpatient hospital care.

Note: If you're in a specialty psychiatric hospital, Medicare only helps pay for a total of 190 days of inpatient care during your lifetime.

Outpatient Mental Health Care: Medicare Part B covers mental health services on an outpatient basis when provided by a doctor, clinical psychologist, clinical social worker, nurse practitioner, clinical nurse specialist, or physician assistant in an office setting, clinic, or hospital outpatient setting.

In 2010, YOU pay 20% of the Medicare-approved amount for visits to a doctor or other health care provider to diagnose your condition or to monitor or change your prescriptions.

In 2010, YOU pay 45% (which is lower than in 2009) of the Medicare-approved amount for outpatient treatment of your conditions (such as counseling or psychotherapy) in a doctor's office setting. This coinsurance amount will continue to decrease over the next 4 years. In a hospital outpatient setting, you pay a copayment.

Mental Health Care (continued)

Partial Hospitalization: Medicare Part B covers partial hospitalization in some cases. It's a structured program of outpatient active psychiatric treatment that is more intense than the care you get in your doctor's or therapist's office. To be eligible for a partial hospitalization program, a doctor must certify that you would otherwise need inpatient treatment.

> **In 2010, YOU pay** a percentage of the Medicare-approved amount for each service you get from a qualified professional (as described above in "Outpatient Mental Health Care"). You also pay 20% of the Medicare-approved amount for each day of service when provided in a hospital outpatient setting or community mental health center.

Non-Doctor Services

Medicare Part B covers certain services provided by health care professionals who aren't doctors such as clinical social workers, nurse practitioners, and physician assistants.

> **In 2010, YOU pay** 20% of the Medicare-approved amount.

Nursing Home Care

Most nursing home care is custodial care (such as help with bathing or dressing). Medicare doesn't cover custodial care if that's the only care you need. However, if it's medically necessary for you to have skilled care (like changing sterile dressings), Medicare Part A will pay for care given in a certified skilled nursing facility (SNF). See Skilled Nursing Facility (SNF) Care on pages 36–38.

Blue words in the text are defined on pages 49–51.

Nutrition Therapy Services (Medical)

Medicare Part B covers medical nutrition therapy services, when ordered by a doctor, for people with kidney disease (but who aren't on dialysis), people who have a kidney transplant, or people with diabetes. If you get dialysis in a dialysis facility, Medicare covers medical nutrition therapy as part of your overall dialysis care.

A registered dietitian or Medicare-approved nutrition professional can give these services. Services may include nutritional assessment, one-on-one counseling, and therapy through an interactive telecommunications system. See Diabetes Supplies and Services on pages 13–15.

In 2010, YOU pay 20% of the Medicare-approved amount.

Occupational Therapy

See Physical Therapy/Occupational Therapy/Speech-Language Pathology on page 30.

Orthotics

Medicare Part B covers artificial limbs and eyes, and arm, leg, back, and neck braces. Medicare doesn't pay for orthopedic shoes unless they're a necessary part of the leg brace. Medicare doesn't pay for dental plates or other dental devices. See Diabetes Supplies and Services (Therapeutic Shoes) on page 14. You must go to a supplier that is enrolled in Medicare for Medicare to cover your orthotics.

In 2010, YOU pay 20% of the Medicare-approved amount.

Ostomy Supplies

Medicare Part B covers ostomy supplies for people who have had a colostomy, ileostomy, or urinary ostomy. Medicare covers the amount of supplies your doctor says you need, based on your condition.

In 2010, YOU pay 20% of the Medicare-approved amount for the doctor's services and supplies.

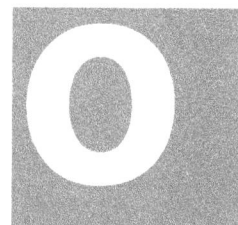

Outpatient Hospital Services

Medicare Part B covers medically-necessary services you get as an outpatient from a Medicare-participating hospital for diagnosis or treatment of an illness or injury. Covered outpatient hospital services include the following:

- Services in an emergency department or outpatient clinic, including same-day surgery
- Laboratory tests billed by the hospital
- Mental health care in a partial-hospitalization program, if a doctor certifies that inpatient treatment would be required without it
- X-rays and other radiology services billed by the hospital
- Medical supplies such as splints and casts
- Screenings and preventive services
- Certain drugs and biologicals that you can't give yourself

    In 2010, YOU pay 20% of the Medicare-approved amount for the doctor's services. For other than doctors' services, you pay a copayment for each service you get in an outpatient hospital setting.

Oxygen Therapy

Medicare Part B covers the rental of oxygen equipment. If you own your own equipment, Medicare will help pay for oxygen contents and supplies for the delivery of oxygen when all of the conditions below are met:

- Your doctor says you have a severe lung disease, or you're not getting enough oxygen.
- You might improve with oxygen therapy.
- Your arterial blood gas level falls within a certain range.
- Other alternative measures have failed.

Under the above conditions Medicare helps pay for the following:

- Systems for furnishing oxygen
- Containers that store oxygen
- Tubing and related supplies for the delivery of oxygen, and oxygen contents

    In 2010, YOU pay 20% of the Medicare-approved amount.

Blue words in the text are defined on pages 49–51.

Pap Test/Pelvic Exam (Screening)

Medicare Part B covers Pap tests and pelvic exams (and a clinical breast exam) for all women once every 24 months. Medicare covers this test and exam once every 12 months if you're at high risk for cervical or vaginal cancer or if you're of childbearing age and have had an abnormal Pap test in the past 36 months.

> **In 2010, YOU pay** $0 for the lab Pap test. You pay 20% of the Medicare-approved amount for the part of the exam when the doctor or other health care provider collects the specimen and for the pelvic exam. If the pelvic exam was provided in a hospital outpatient setting, you pay a copayment. If you have your Pap test, pelvic exam, and clinical breast exam in the same visit as a routine physical exam, you must pay for the physical exam.

Physical Exams (one-time "Welcome to Medicare" physical exam)

Medicare Part B covers a one-time "Welcome to Medicare" physical exam, which includes a review of your health, as well as education and counseling about the preventive services you need (including certain screenings and shots), and referrals for other care if needed. Medicare doesn't cover routine physical exams.

Important: You must have the physical exam within the first 12 months you have Medicare Part B. When you make your appointment, let your doctor's office know you would like to schedule your "Welcome to Medicare" physical exam. The Part B deductible doesn't apply.

> **In 2010, YOU pay** 100% for most routine physical exams. You pay 20% of the Medicare-approved amount for the "Welcome to Medicare" physical exam for the doctor's services. In a hospital outpatient setting, you pay a copayment.

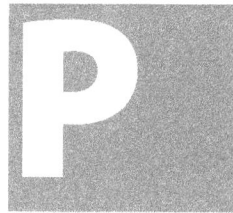

Physical Therapy/Occupational Therapy/Speech-Language Pathology Services

Medicare Part B helps pay for medically-necessary outpatient physical and occupational therapy and speech-language pathology services when both of these conditions are met:

- Your doctor or therapist sets up the plan of treatment.
- Your doctor periodically reviews the plan to see how long you will need therapy.

You can get outpatient physical therapy/occupational therapy/speech-language pathology services from a Medicare-approved outpatient provider such as a participating hospital or skilled nursing facility, or from a participating home health agency, rehabilitation agency, or a comprehensive outpatient rehabilitation facility. Also, you can get services from a Medicare-approved physical or occupational therapist, in private practice, in his or her office, or in your home. Medicare doesn't pay for services given by a speech-language pathologist in private practice. In 2010, there may be limits on physical therapy, occupational therapy, and speech-language pathology services. If so, there may be exceptions to these limits.

In 2010, YOU pay 20% of the Medicare-approved amount.

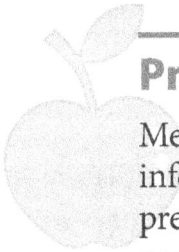

Pneumococcal Shot

Medicare Part B covers a pneumococcal shot to help prevent pneumococcal infections (like certain types of pneumonia). Most people only need this preventive shot once in their lifetime. Talk with your doctor to see if you need this shot.

In 2010, YOU pay $0 for a pneumococcal shot if the doctor or supplier accepts assignment for giving the shot.

Blue words in the text are defined on pages 49-51.

Section 1: List of What Original Medicare Covers

Prescription Drugs (Outpatient) Limited Coverage

Part B covers a limited number of outpatient prescription drugs, and only under limited conditions. Generally these include drugs you would not usually give to yourself, that you get at a doctor's office or hospital outpatient setting. Doctors and pharmacies must accept assignment for Part B drugs, so you should never be asked to pay more than the coinsurance or copayment for the drug itself.

The following are examples of drugs covered by Part B:

- **Infused Drugs:** Medicare covers drugs infused through an item of durable medical equipment, such as an infusion pump or nebulizer if considered reasonable and necessary.

- **Some Antigens:** Medicare will help pay for antigens if they're prepared by a provider and given by a properly-instructed person (who could be the patient) under appropriate supervision.

- **Injectable Osteoporosis Drugs:** Medicare helps pay for an injectable drug for osteoporosis for certain women with Medicare. See note for women with osteoporosis under Home Health Services on pages 21–22.

- **Erythropoisis–stimulating Agents:** Medicare will help pay for erythropoietin by injection if you have End-Stage Renal Disease (permanent kidney failure requiring dialysis or a kidney transplant) or need this drug to treat anemia related to certain other conditions.

- **Blood Clotting Factors:** If you have hemophilia, Medicare will help pay for clotting factors you give yourself by injection.

- **Injectable Drugs:** Medicare covers most injectable drugs given by a licensed medical provider, if the drug is considered reasonable and necessary for treatment.

- **Immunosuppressive Drugs:** Medicare covers immunosuppressive drug therapy for transplant patients if the transplant meets Medicare coverage requirements, the patient is enrolled in Part A at the time of the transplant, and the patient is enrolled in Medicare Part B at the time the drugs are dispensed.

  Note: Medicare drug plans may cover immunosuppressive drugs, even if Medicare or an employer or union group health plan didn't pay for the transplant.

Prescription Drugs (Outpatient) Limited Coverage (continued)

The following are examples of drugs covered by Part B (continued):

- **Oral Cancer Drugs:** Medicare will help pay for some cancer drugs you take by mouth if the same drug is available in injectable form. Currently, Medicare covers the following cancer drugs you take by mouth:

  - Capecitabine (Xeloda®)
  - Busulfan (Myleran®)
  - Cyclophosphamide (Cytoxan®)
  - Etoposide (VePesid®)
  - Melphalan (Alkeran®)
  - Temozolomide (Temodar®)
  - Topotecan (Hycamtin®)
  - Methotrexate (Rheumatrex®, Trexall®)

  Medicare may cover new cancer drugs as they become available.

- **Oral Anti-Nausea Drugs:** Medicare will help pay for oral anti-nausea drugs used as part of an anti-cancer chemotherapeutic regimen. The drugs must be administered immediately before, at, or within 48 hours and must be used as a full therapeutic replacement for the intravenous anti-nausea drugs that would otherwise be given.

  In 2010, YOU pay 20% of the Medicare-approved amount for covered Part B prescription drugs that you get in a doctor's office or pharmacy. In a hospital outpatient setting, you pay a copayment. However, if you get drugs in a hospital outpatient setting that aren't covered under Part B, you pay 100% for the drugs unless you have Part D or other prescription drug coverage. In that case, what you pay depends on whether your drug plan covers the drug, and whether the hospital is in your drug plan's network. Contact your prescription drug plan to find out what you pay for drugs you get in a hospital outpatient setting.

Blue words in the text are defined on pages 49–51.

Section 1: List of What Original Medicare Covers

Preventive Services

Medicare Part B covers the following preventive and screening services that may help prevent illness or detect illness at an early stage, when treatment is likely to work best:

- Abdominal Aortic Aneurysm Screening on page 6
- Bone Mass Measurement on page 8
- Cardiovascular Disease Screenings on page 9
- Colorectal Cancer Screening on pages 10–11
- Diabetes Screening on page 13
- Diabetes Self-Management Training on page 14
- Glaucoma Tests on page 20
- HIV Screening on page 21
- Mammogram (screening) on page 25
- Medical Nutrition Therapy Services on page 27
- One-time "Welcome to Medicare" physical exam on page 29
- Pap Test/Pelvic Exam (screening) on page 29
- Prostate Cancer Screening on page 33
- Shots including the following:
    - Flu Shot on page 19
    - Pneumococcal Shot on page 30
    - Hepatitis B Shot on page 21
- Smoking Cessation Counseling on page 38

    In 2010, YOU pay the cost listed on the page for that specific service.

Prostate Cancer Screenings

Medicare Part B covers prostate cancer screening tests once every 12 months for men with Medicare who are 50 and older. Coverage begins the day after your 50th birthday. Covered tests include the following:

Digital Rectal Examination

In 2010, YOU pay generally, 20% of the Medicare-approved amount for the digital rectal exam for the doctor's services. In a hospital outpatient setting, you pay a copayment.

Prostate Specific Antigen (PSA) Test

In 2010, YOU pay $0 for the PSA test.

Prosthetic Devices

Medicare Part B covers prosthetic devices needed to replace an internal body part or function. These include Medicare-approved corrective lenses needed after a cataract operation (see Eyeglasses/Contact Lenses on page 19), ostomy bags and certain related supplies (see Ostomy Supplies on page 27), and breast prostheses (including a surgical bra) after a mastectomy (see Breast Prosthesis on page 8). You must go to a supplier that's enrolled in Medicare for Medicare to pay for your device. Medicare Part A or Medicare Part B covers surgically implanted prosthetic devices depending on whether the surgery takes place in an inpatient or outpatient setting.

> **In 2010, YOU pay** 20% of the Medicare-approved amount for external prosthetic devices. For surgeries to implant prosthetic devices in a hospital inpatient setting covered under Part A, see Hospital Care (Inpatient) on page 23. For surgeries to implant prosthetic devices in a hospital outpatient setting covered under Part B, see Outpatient Hospital Services on page 28.

Pulmonary Rehabilitation

Starting January 1, 2010, Medicare covers a comprehensive program of pulmonary rehabilitation if you have moderate to very severe chronic obstructive pulmonary disease (COPD) and have a referral for pulmonary rehabilitation from the doctor treating your chronic respiratory disease. These services are intended to help you breathe better, make you stronger, and able to live more independently. These services may be provided in doctors' offices or hospital outpatient setting that offer pulmonary rehabilitation programs.

Blue words in the text are defined on pages 49–51.

> **In 2010, YOU pay** 20% of the Medicare-approved amount if you get the service in a doctor's office. You pay a copayment per session if you get the service in a hospital outpatient setting.

R Radiation Therapy

Medicare Part A covers radiation therapy for patients who are hospital inpatients. Medicare Part B covers it for outpatients or patients in freestanding clinics.

> **In 2010, YOU pay** the inpatient deductible and coinsurance (if applicable).

> **In 2010, YOU pay** a set copayment (for outpatient radiation therapy).

> **In 2010, YOU pay** 20% of the Medicare-approved amount for radiation therapy at a freestanding facility.

Religious Nonmedical Health Care Institution (RNHCI)

Medicare doesn't cover the religious portion of RNHCI care. Specifically, Medicare Part A covers inpatient nonreligious nonmedical care when the following conditions are met:

- The RNHCI has agreed and is currently certified to participate in Medicare.
- The Utilization Review Committee agrees that you would require hospital or skilled nursing facility care if it weren't for your religious beliefs.
- You have a written election on file with Medicare indicating that your need for RNHCI care is based on your religious beliefs. The election must also indicate that if you decide to accept standard medical care, you will cancel the election and may have to wait 1 to 5 years to be eligible for a new election to get RNHCI services. Please note that you're always able to get medically-necessary Medicare Part A services.

   In 2010, for each benefit period **YOU pay** the following:
   Days 1 - 60: $1,100 deductible
   Days 61 - 90: $275 coinsurance each day
   Days 91 - 150: $550 coinsurance each day
   Beyond 150 days: all costs
   For information about benefit periods and lifetime reserve days, see pages 49–50.

Respite Care (Inpatient)

Medicare Part A covers respite care (inpatient care given to a hospice patient so that the usual caregiver can rest) for hospice patients. See Hospice Care on pages 22–23.

   In 2010, YOU pay 5% of the Medicare-approved amount.

Rural Health Clinic and Federally-Qualified Health Center Services

Medicare Part B covers a broad range of outpatient primary care services.

   In 2010, YOU pay 20% of the Medicare-approved amount.

Second Surgical Opinions

Medicare Part B covers a second opinion in some cases for surgery that isn't an emergency. A second opinion is when another doctor gives his or her view about your health problem and how it should be treated. Medicare will also help pay for a third opinion if the first and second opinions are different.

In 2010, YOU pay 20% of the Medicare-approved amount.

Shots (Vaccinations)

Medicare covers the following shots:

- **Flu Shot** on page 19
- **Hepatitis B Shot** on page 21
- **Pneumococcal Shot** on page 30

Skilled Nursing Facility (SNF) Care

Medicare Part A covers skilled care in a skilled nursing facility (SNF) under certain conditions for a limited time. Skilled care is health care given when you need skilled nursing or rehabilitation staff to manage, observe, and evaluate your care. Medicare covers certain skilled care services that are needed daily on a short-term basis (up to 100 days).

In 2010, YOU pay the following for each benefit period (following at least a related 3-day covered hospital stay):

Days 1 - 20: $0 each day

Days 21 - 100: up to $137.50 each day

Beyond 100 days: 100%

There's a limit of 100 days of Medicare Part A SNF coverage in each benefit period.

Blue words in the text are defined on pages 49–51.

Skilled Nursing Facility (SNF) Care (continued)

Medicare will cover skilled nursing facility care if all these conditions are met:

1. You have Medicare Part A and have days left in your benefit period to use.

2. You have a qualifying hospital stay. This means an inpatient hospital stay of 3 consecutive days or more, including the day you're admitted to the hospital, but not including the day you leave the hospital.

Note: Time that you spend in a hospital as an outpatient before you're admitted doesn't count toward the 3 inpatient days you need to have a qualifying hospital stay for SNF benefit purposes.

You must enter the SNF within a short time (generally 30 days) of leaving the hospital and require skilled services related to your hospital stay. See item 5. After you leave the SNF, if you re-enter the same or another SNF within 30 days, you don't need another 3-day qualifying hospital stay to get additional SNF benefits. This is also true if you stop getting skilled care while in the SNF and then start getting skilled care again within 30 days.

3. Your doctor has decided that you need daily skilled care. It must be given by, or under the direct supervision of, skilled nursing or rehabilitation staff. If you're in the SNF for skilled rehabilitation services only, your care is considered daily care even if these therapy services are offered just 5 or 6 days a week, as long as you need and get the therapy services each day they're offered.

4. You get these skilled services in a SNF that is certified by Medicare.

5. You need these skilled services for a medical condition that was either of the following:
   – A hospital-related medical condition (any condition that was treated during your qualifying 3-day hospital stay, even if it wasn't the reason you were admitted to the hospital).
   – A condition that started while you were getting care in the SNF for a hospital-related medical condition. For example, if while you're getting SNF care for a stroke that was also treated during your qualifying 3-day hospital stay, you develop an infection that requires IV antibiotics, Medicare will cover your SNF care for treating the infection (as long as you also meet the conditions listed in items 1–4).

Skilled Nursing Facility (SNF) Care (continued)

While you're in a non-covered stay in the Medicare-certified part of the facility, your Part B therapy services (physical therapy, occupational therapy, and speech-language pathology) must be billed by the facility. No other therapy service may be billed by another setting, such as an outpatient hospital setting. If you leave the Medicare-certified part of the facility, your therapy services in the non-Medicare-certified part of the facility are limited by a specific dollar amount each year unless you get the services from an outpatient hospital setting.

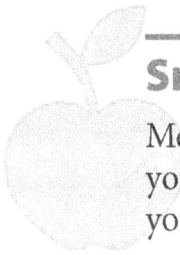

Smoking Cessation (counseling to stop smoking)

Medicare Part B covers up to 8 face-to-face visits in a 12-month period if you're diagnosed with an illness caused or complicated by tobacco use, or you take a medicine that's affected by tobacco.

In 2010, YOU pay 20% of the Medicare-approved amount for the doctor's services. In a hospital outpatient setting, you pay a copayment.

Speech-Language Pathology

See Physical Therapy/Occupational Therapy/Speech-Language Pathology on page 30.

Substance-Related Disorders

Medicare covers treatment for substance-related disorders in inpatient or outpatient settings. Certain limits apply. See Mental Health Care (Inpatient or Outpatient) on pages 25–26.

Supplies (you use at home)

Medicare Part B generally doesn't cover common medical supplies like bandages and gauze. Medicare covers some diabetes and dialysis supplies. See Diabetes Supplies and Services on pages 13–15 and Dialysis (Kidney) on page 16. For items such as walkers, oxygen, and wheelchairs, see Durable Medical Equipment on pages 17–18.

In 2010, YOU pay 100% for most common medical supplies you use at home.

Blue words in the text are defined on pages 49–51.

Surgical Dressing Services

Medicare Part B covers medically-necessary treatment of a surgical or surgically-treated wound.

In 2010, YOU pay 20% of the Medicare-approved amount for the doctor's services. You pay a copayment for these services when you get them in a hospital outpatient setting. You pay nothing for the supplies.

Telehealth

Medicare Part B covers certain telehealth services, like office visits and consultations that are provided using an interactive two-way telecommunications system (like real-time audio and video) by an eligible provider who is at a location different from the patient's. Telehealth is available in some rural areas, under certain conditions, and only if the patient is located at one of the following places: a doctor's office, hospital, rural health clinic, federally-qualified health center, hospital-based dialysis facility, skilled nursing facility, or community mental health center.

In 2010, YOU pay 20% of the Medicare-approved amount for the doctor's services.

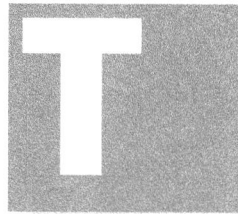

Therapeutic Shoes

See Diabetes Supplies and Services (Therapeutic Shoes) on page 14.

Transplants (Doctor Services)

Medicare Part B covers doctor services for transplants. See Transplants (Facility Charges) on page 40.

In 2010, YOU pay 20% of the Medicare-approved amount for doctor services.

Transplants (Facility Charges)

Medicare Part A covers transplants of the heart, lung, kidney, pancreas, intestine, and liver under certain conditions and only at Medicare-approved facilities. Medicare only approves facilities for kidney, heart, liver, lung, intestine, and some pancreas transplants. Medicare Part B covers cornea and bone marrow transplants. Bone marrow and cornea transplants aren't limited to approved facilities.

Transplant coverage includes necessary tests, labs, and exams before surgery. It also includes immunosuppressive drugs (under certain conditions), follow-up care for you, and procurement of organs and tissues. Medicare pays for the costs for a living donor for a kidney transplant.

In 2010, YOU pay various amounts. For inpatient transplants, see Hospital Care (Inpatient) on page 23.

Transportation (Routine)

Medicare doesn't cover transportation to get routine health care. For more information, see Ambulance Services on page 6.

Travel (health care needed when traveling outside the United States)

Medicare generally doesn't cover health care while you're traveling outside the United States. Puerto Rico, the U.S. Virgin Islands, Guam, American Samoa, and the Northern Mariana Islands are considered part of the United States. There are some exceptions. In some cases, Medicare Part B may pay for services that you get while on board a ship within the territorial waters adjoining the land areas of the United States. In rare cases, Medicare Part A may pay for inpatient hospital services that you get in a foreign country under the following circumstances:

- You're in the United States when a medical emergency occurs, and the foreign hospital is closer than the nearest United States hospital that can treat the emergency.
- You're traveling through Canada without unreasonable delay by the most direct route between Alaska and another state when a medical emergency occurs, and the Canadian hospital is closer than the nearest United States hospital that can treat the emergency.

Blue words in the text are defined on pages 49–51.

Travel (health care needed when traveling outside the United States) (continued)

- You live in the United States and the foreign hospital is closer to your home than the nearest United States hospital that can treat your medical condition, regardless of whether an emergency exists.

Medicare also pays for doctor and ambulance services you get in a foreign country as part of a covered inpatient hospital stay.

In 2010, YOU pay 100% of charges, in most cases. In the situations described above, you pay the part of the charge that you would normally pay for covered services.

Urgently-Needed Care

Medicare Part B covers this care to treat a sudden illness or injury that isn't a medical emergency.

In 2010, YOU pay 20% of the Medicare-approved amount.

Walker/Wheelchair

Medicare Part B covers power-operated vehicles (scooters), walkers, and wheelchairs as durable medical equipment that your doctor prescribes for use in your home. For more information, see Durable Medical Equipment on pages 17–18.

Power Wheelchair: You must have a face-to-face examination and a written prescription from a doctor or other treating provider before Medicare helps pay for a power wheelchair.

In 2010, YOU pay 20% of the Medicare-approved amount.

X-rays

Medicare Part B covers medically-necessary diagnostic X-rays that are ordered by your treating doctor. For more information, see Diagnostic Tests on page 15.

In 2010, YOU pay 20% of the Medicare-approved amount. In a hospital outpatient setting, you pay a copayment.

Notes

_____

_____

_____

_____

_____

_____

_____

_____

_____

_____

_____

_____

_____

_____

_____

_____

_____

_____

_____

For More Information

Visit MyMedicare.gov for Personalized Information

Register at www.MyMedicare.gov, Medicare's secure online service for accessing your personal Medicare information. You can use this site to do any of the following:

- Complete your Initial Enrollment Questionnaire so your bills get paid correctly.
- Track your health care claims.
- Check your Part B deductible status.
- View your eligibility information.
- Track the preventive services you can get.
- Find a Medicare health plan or Medicare Prescription Drug Plan.
- Keep your Medicare information in one convenient place.
- Sign up to get your "Medicare & You" handbook electronically.

Visit www.medicare.gov for General Information about Medicare

You can do the following:

- See what Medicare plans are available in your area.
- Find doctors who accept Medicare.
- See what Medicare covers, including preventive services.
- Get Medicare appeals information and forms.
- Get information on the quality of care provided by nursing homes, hospitals, home health agencies, plans, and dialysis facilities.
- Look up helpful telephone numbers for your area.
- View Medicare publications.

Blue words in the text are defined on pages 49–51.

Section 2: For More Information

Call 1-800-MEDICARE for Answers to Your Medicare Questions

The 1-800-MEDICARE (1-800-633-4227) helpline has a speech-automated system to make it easier for you to get the information you need 24 hours a day, including weekends. The system will ask you questions to direct your call automatically. Speak clearly, call from a quiet area, and have your Medicare card in front of you. If you need help, you can say "Agent" at any time to talk to a customer service representative. TTY users should call 1-877-486-2048.

Note: If you want Medicare to give your personal health information to someone other than you, you need to let Medicare know in writing. You can fill out a "Medicare Authorization to Disclose Personal Health Information" form. You can do this online by visiting www.medicare.gov/MedicareOnlineForms/PublicForms/CMS10106.pdf or calling 1-800-MEDICARE to get a copy of the form.

Free Publications About Medicare and Related Topics

Health care decisions are important. Medicare provides information to help you make informed decisions. Detailed booklets and fact sheets are available on various Medicare topics. Here's how to get free publications:

- **View or print electronic copies** on www.medicare.gov under "Find a Medicare Publication" by doing any of the following:
    - Search by keyword (such as "rights" or "mental health").
    - Select "View All Medicare Publications."
    - See below for links to specific publications on many topics mentioned in this booklet.

- **Order printed copies** to be mailed to you:
    - Visit www.medicare.gov. If the publication you want has a check box after "Order Publication," you can order it.
    - Call 1-800-MEDICARE. Say "Publications" to find out if a copy is available.

Ambulance coverage

"Medicare Coverage of Ambulance Services"
www.medicare.gov/Publications/Pubs/pdf/11021.pdf

Comparing plans and health care providers

- "Guide to Choosing a Nursing Home"
www.medicare.gov/Publications/Pubs/pdf/02174.pdf
- "Use Information about Quality on Medicare.gov"
www.medicare.gov/Publications/Pubs/pdf/11266.pdf

Free Publications About Medicare and Related Topics (continued)

Coverage outside the U.S. (Travel)

"Medicare Coverage Outside the United States"
www.medicare.gov/Publications/Pubs/pdf/11037.pdf

Diabetes

"Medicare Coverage of Diabetes Supplies and Services"
www.medicare.gov/Publications/Pubs/pdf/11022.pdf

Durable Medical Equipment (DME)

"Medicare Coverage of Durable Medical Equipment and Other Devices"
www.medicare.gov/Publications/Pubs/pdf/11045.pdf

Home health care

"Medicare and Home Health Care"
www.medicare.gov/Publications/Pubs/pdf/10969.pdf

Hospice care

"Medicare Hospice Benefits"
www.medicare.gov/Publications/Pubs/pdf/02154.pdf

Hospital care

"Are You a Hospital Inpatient or Outpatient? If You Have Medicare-Ask!"
www.medicare.gov/Publications/Pubs/pdf/11435.pdf

Kidney dialysis and transplant services

"Medicare Coverage of Kidney Dialysis and Kidney Transplant Services"
www.medicare.gov/Publications/Pubs/pdf/10128.pdf

Medicare prescription drug coverage

"Your Guide to Medicare Prescription Drug Coverage"
www.medicare.gov/Publications/Pubs/pdf/11109.pdf

Mental health care

"Medicare and Your Mental Health Benefits"
www.medicare.gov/Publications/Pubs/pdf/10184.pdf

Preventive services

"Your Guide to Medicare's Preventive Services"
www.medicare.gov/Publications/Pubs/pdf/10110.pdf

Section 2: For More Information

Free Publications About Medicare and Related Topics (continued)

Skilled nursing care

"Medicare Coverage of Skilled Nursing Facility Care"
www.medicare.gov/Publications/Pubs/pdf/10153.pdf

Rights and protections

"Your Medicare Rights and Protections"
www.medicare.gov/Publications/Pubs/pdf/10112.pdf

Do you help someone with Medicare?

Medicare has two new resources to help you get the information you need:

- Visit www.medicare.gov/caregivers to help someone with Medicare choose a drug plan, compare nursing homes, get help with billing, and more.

- Sign up for the free bi-monthly "Ask Medicare" electronic newsletter (e-Newsletter) when you go to the site mentioned above. The e-Newsletter has the latest information including important dates, Medicare changes, and resources in your community.

Section 2: For More Information

Other Important Contacts

Below are telephone numbers for organizations that provide nationwide services.

State Health Insurance Assistance Program (SHIP) Call for free personalized health insurance counseling, including help making health care decisions, information on programs for people with limited income and resources, and help with claims, billing, and appeals.	Call 1-800-MEDICARE (1-800-633-4227) for telephone number. TTY users should call 1-877-486-2048.
Social Security Call for a replacement Medicare card; address or name changes; for information about Medicare Part A and/or Part B eligibility, entitlement, and enrollment; to apply for Extra Help with Medicare prescription drug costs; and to report a death.	1-800-772-1213 TTY 1-800-325-0778
Coordination of Benefits Contractor Call for information on whether Medicare or your other insurance pays first.	1-800-999-1118 TTY 1-800-318-8782
Department of Defense Call for questions about TRICARE for Life.	TRICARE for Life 1-866-773-0404 TTY 1-866-773-0405
Department of Health and Human Services Office of Inspector General Call if you suspect billing fraud.	1-800-447-8477 TTY 1-800-377-4950
Office for Civil Rights Call if you think you were discriminated against or if your health information privacy rights were violated.	1-800-368-1019 TTY 1-800-537-7697
Department of Veterans Affairs Call if you're a veteran or have served in the U.S. military.	1-800-827-1000 TTY 1-800-829-4833
Railroad Retirement Board (RRB) Call if you get RRB benefits and have questions about benefits, address or name changes, death notification, to enroll in Medicare, or to replace your Medicare card.	Call your local RRB office or 1-877-772-5772.

Notes

Words to Know

Ambulatory Surgical Center—A facility where simpler surgeries are performed for patients who aren't expected to need more than 24 hours of care.

Appeal— An appeal is the action you can take if you disagree with a coverage or payment decision made by Medicare, your Medicare health plan, or your Medicare Prescription Drug Plan. You can appeal if Medicare or your plan denies one of the following:

- Your request for a health care service, supply, or prescription that you think you should be able to get
- Your request for payment for health care or a prescription drug you already got
- Your request to change the amount you must pay for a prescription drug

You can also appeal if you are already getting coverage and Medicare or your plan stops paying.

Assignment—An agreement by your doctor to be paid directly by Medicare, to accept the payment amount Medicare approves for the service, and not to bill you for any more than the Medicare deductible and coinsurance.

Benefit Period— The way that Original Medicare measures your use of hospital and skilled nursing facility (SNF) services. A benefit period begins the day you go to a hospital or skilled nursing facility. The benefit period ends when you haven't received any inpatient hospital care (or skilled care in a SNF) for 60 days in a row. If you go into a hospital or a skilled nursing facility after one benefit period has ended, a new benefit period begins. You must pay the inpatient hospital deductible for each benefit period. There is no limit to the number of benefit periods.

Coinsurance— An amount you may be required to pay as your share of the cost for services after you pay any deductibles. Coinsurance is usually a percentage (for example, 20%).

Section 3: Words to Know

Copayment—An amount you may be required to pay as your share of the cost for a medical service or supply, like a doctor's visit or a prescription. A copayment is usually a set amount, rather than a percentage. For example, you might pay $10 or $20 for a doctor's visit or prescription.

Critical Access Hospital—A small facility that provides outpatient services, as well as inpatient services on a limited basis, to people in rural areas and is designated as a critical access hospital by Medicare.

Deductible— The amount you must pay for health care or prescriptions, before Original Medicare, your prescription drug plan, or your other insurance begins to pay.

Lifetime Reserve Days—In Original Medicare, these are additional days that Medicare will pay for when you are in a hospital for more than 90 days. You have a total of 60 reserve days that can be used during your lifetime. For each lifetime reserve day, Medicare pays all covered costs except for a daily coinsurance ($550 in 2010).

Medically Necessary— Services or supplies that are needed for the diagnosis or treatment of your medical condition and meet accepted standards of medical practice.

Medicare Advantage Plan (Part C)—A type of Medicare health plan offered by a private company that contracts with Medicare to provide you with all your Medicare Part A and Part B benefits. Medicare Advantage Plans include Health Maintenance Organizations, Preferred Provider Organizations, Private Fee-for-Service Plans, Special Needs Plans, and Medicare Medical Savings Account Plans. If you are enrolled in a Medicare Advantage Plan, Medicare services are covered through the plan and aren't paid for under Original Medicare. Most Medicare Advantage Plans offer prescription drug coverage.

Medicare-Approved Amount— In Original Medicare, this is the amount a doctor or supplier that accepts assignment can be paid. It includes what Medicare pays and any deductible, coinsurance, or copayment that you pay. It may be less than the actual amount a doctor or supplier charges.

Section 3: Words to Know

Medicare Health Plan— A Medicare health plan is offered by a private company that contracts with Medicare to provide Part A and Part B benefits to people with Medicare who enroll in the plan.

Medicare Prescription Drug Plan (Part D)—A stand-alone drug plan that adds prescription drug coverage to Original Medicare, some Medicare Cost Plans, some Medicare Private-Fee-for-Service Plans, and Medicare Medical Savings Account Plans. These plans are offered by insurance companies and other private companies approved by Medicare. Medicare Advantage Plans may also offer prescription drug coverage that follows the same rules as Medicare Prescription Drug Plans.

Preventive Services— Health care to prevent illness or detect illness at an early stage, when treatment is likely to work best (for example, preventive services include Pap tests, flu shots, and screening mammograms).

Referral— A written order from your primary care doctor for you to see a specialist or to get certain medical services. In many Health Maintenance Organizations (HMOs), you need to get a referral before you can get medical care from anyone except your primary care doctor. If you don't get a referral first, the plan may not pay for the services.

Religious Nonmedical Health Care Institution (RNHCI)— A facility that provides nonmedical health care items and services to people who need hospital or skilled nursing facility care, but for whom that care would be inconsistent with their religious beliefs.

**U.S. DEPARTMENT OF
HEALTH AND HUMAN SERVICES**

Centers for Medicare & Medicaid Services

7500 Security Boulevard
Baltimore, MD 21244-1850

Official Business
Penalty for Private Use, $300

CMS Product No. 10116
Revised December 2009

Your Medicare Benefits

*My Health.
My Medicare.*

- www.medicare.gov
- 1-800-MEDICARE (1-800-633-4227)
- TTY 1-877-486-2048

¿ Necesita usted una copia en español? Llame GRATIS al
1-800-MEDICARE (1-800-633-4227).

www.ingramcontent.com/pod-product-compliance
Lightning Source LLC
Chambersburg PA
CBHW080253200326

41520CB00022B/7133